Serving with Grace

Serving with Grace

Lay Leadership
as a Spiritual Practice

Erik Walker Wikstrom

Skinner House Books
Boston

Printed in the United States

Cover and text design by Suzanne Morgan

Print ISBN: 978-1-55896-562-1
eBook ISBN: 978-1-55896-580-5

6 5 4
16 15 14 13

Library of Congress Cataloging-in-Publication Data

Wikstrom, Erik Walker.
Serving with grace : lay leadership as a spiritual practice / Erik Walker Wikstrom.
     p. cm.
ISBN-13: 978-1-55896-562-1 (pbk. : alk. paper)
ISBN-10: 1-55896-562-9 (pbk. : alk. paper) 1. Christian leadership.
2. Leadership—Religious aspects—Christianity. 3. Service (Theology)
I. Title.
 BV652.1.W485 2010
 253—dc22
                              2009046606

Contents

To those adults who recognized my ministry when I was a lay youth, and to those laypeople who have ministered with and to me after I was ordained. And of course, as always, to Mary, Theo, and Lester.

Introduction

Common wisdom holds that people come to church for a sense of belonging, and that getting involved with a committee or task force is a great way to meet people and feel more connected. You do meet people while serving on a committee, and, yes, working together in common purpose can create these bonds. But perhaps this is not really why people come to church. Though this is often why they say they come, I think there is an even deeper reason—to have their lives transformed. (In fact, Thomas Bandy argues just this in his book *Kicking Habits*.) If so, then no amount of encouragement will get them to sign up for one more thing in their already busy lives. Just *getting involved* is not enough. It doesn't speak to their deepest need—a transformed life.

Imagine if the practical and administrative work of the church—meetings, planning, teaching, etc.—was understood not as a necessary evil but as an integral part of the mission of the church to spiritually nurture us. What if lay leadership were not a means to an end but an end in itself? Could you experience the meeting room as a zendo and the deliberations of a task force as a form of group prayer? Imagine church not as a place led by a few overly taxed people but one where leadership is a broadly shared ministry that members of the community undertake for the deep joy of it.

Serving with Grace is intended for current and potential lay leaders, to help you understand your work for the church as an integrated aspect of a fully rounded spiritual life. It is intended both for those in typically recognized "leadership roles"—such as Board members, committee chairs, and the like—as well as for those who lead by doing while serving on a committee, teaching religious education, or helping to pull together the holiday fair. Woven throughout are practical, concrete practices you can do alone or in a group to reinforce the theory. As the old saying goes, it is far easier for us to act ourselves into a new way of thinking than it is to think ourselves into a new way of acting. These practices will give you tools to relate to your leadership roles in new ways. And the new behaviors that result will, in time, help transform the roles themselves. These tips and techniques will help you to bring together what may have felt like two distinct aspects of church life—your work as a leader and your own spiritual development. They do not require any particular theological or philosophical understandings. They are practices anyone can engage with and will only be deepened by the colors and textures of your own religious perspectives.

In his classic *Everyday Spiritual Practice*, Scott Alexander boldly asserts that the purpose of spiritual practice is to "examine, shape, and care for your life—and the life around you—to achieve more wholeness, satisfaction, depth, and meaning." The goal of this book is not only to help you become a more effective leader who is less likely to burn out; it is also to help you understand lay leadership as its own spiritual practice, which can stretch you in new directions. This practice calls you to live out your Principles in a community that shares them. It calls you to develop and strengthen spiritual virtues that will carry forward into the rest of your life. Learning to see the holy in the troublesome committee member who objects to everything may lead you to regard your neighbor, your co-worker, or your children in a new light. Learning enough about yourself to decide which church tasks to take on and which to decline may mean truly appreciating all your strengths and weaknesses for the first time.

The question to you is: Will you accept the challenge and invitation? Will you take advantage of the opportunity to use your service in the church to deepen your spiritual life and further your spiritual journey? The monasteries and intentional spiritual communities of all religious traditions understand that each and every moment of each and every day provides opportunities to learn, deepen, and grow. Whether sitting in meditation and prayer in your room or chopping carrots and washing dishes in the kitchen—anything can be used as a tool for deepening our connection with life. The quiet of the prayer bench and the bustle of the business office are not seen as two distinct things—they are two aspects of the same process. The busy work of the monastery provides as much of a pathway as the time of prayer. And when the work is seen that way, that's just what it does.

The Spirituality of Service

The most superficial and practical reason to become a leader is that your church needs you. Our congregations are voluntary associations and depend on donations—not just of our financial resources but of our time and talents as well. In fact, even if our members pledged sufficient financial support such that every single task could be farmed out to paid employees, the church would still need volunteers because that's the nature of the voluntary association.

We also get involved in leadership because it feels good. We meet people and form friendships, becoming more fully integrated into the community. Some of us stop there, of course, satisfying our own need for a sense of belonging, yet at this point there is also a doorway to service as a spiritual practice. As Rev. Gary Kowalski put it in a sermon,

> People who come to Unitarian Universalism seeking spiritual goods are likely to be disappointed so long as they have the outlook of consumers in search of material goods. If their connection to

our liberal faith is to grow into something more rewarding, they have to give up the consumer mind set and begin to think of themselves instead as shareholders, investors, co-owners in what happens in church. Just as the parties in a marriage see themselves as partners rather than competitors with a joint share in the success of the enterprise.

There may be more challenges inherent in serving as a leader in your church than, say, in volunteering once a month in a local soup kitchen, which is not also your spiritual community and where you do not also have other kinds of ties and relationships to complicate things. Yet the greater the challenges, perhaps, the greater the rewards. Service within the context of your church means working with a group of people who understand your Unitarian Universalist values and commitments and will hold you accountable to them.

The metaphor of a marriage may seem at first an odd one for lay leadership. Who wants to be "married" to their church? Yet we often describe our congregations as "families," and few of us were born into them, so perhaps the metaphor is more apt than at first it seemed. Like a marriage, we choose these relationships. And the metaphor points out the spiritual as well as practical dimensions of these relationships. Spiritually healthy couples who enter into a lifelong commitment do so with the understanding that they will share the work necessary to maintain their partnership. They will make decisions together, sometimes fight, speak truth to each other in love, make sacrifices for each other, and go through life with the awareness that they are each responsible for something larger than either alone. The upside of all this work is the forging of a relationship that is tested and sturdy, one that can support either partner when times are hard. At our best, we don't require congregants to "earn" our care and compassion, but a congregant who has worked with her fellow community members in common cause is more likely to have developed strong relationships and a sense of belonging in the community. More than someone who simply attends worship every Sunday, a lay leader who knows that he has given so much of himself to the church can feel comfortable accepting support and help when he needs it.

Also, active participation in the life of your spiritual community gives you an acknowledged stake in it, empowering you to make that community your true spiritual home by infusing it with your values. Committee meetings and fundraisers may seem far removed from the message of the Sunday morning sermon, but it is here that your congregation literally practices what it preaches, or doesn't. Lay work is a natural complement to worship, the opportunity to act upon and test your Unitarian Universalist values. Rev. Alice Blair Wesley writes, "Show me the patterns of your church organization, and I'll show you what the people of the church find worthiest of their loyalty. Organization and theology are not two different things. Our organization is a function of our actual theology." As a lay leader, you influence that organization, and that makes you a co-creator of the church's communal theology.

Every religious tradition teaches the value of giving service as an end in itself. Even Twelve Step programs and secular psychologies have discovered the profound effect that doing good for others has on oneself. Albert Schweitzer once said, "I don't know what your destiny will be, but one thing I know. The only ones among you who will be truly happy will be those who have sought and found how to serve." Fundamentally, serving your church is simply another form of service. In her book *Blessing the World*, Rebecca Parker quotes a member of her congregation explaining why he tithes. His insight applies equally well to giving time and energy to the church instead of money:

> To tithe is to tell the truth about who I am. If I did not tithe, it would say that I was a person who had nothing to give, a person who had received nothing from life. A person who did not matter to the larger society or whose life's meaning was in providing for his own needs alone. But in fact, who I am is the opposite of all of these things. I am a person who has something to give. I am a person who has received abundantly from life. I am a person whose presence matters in the world, and I am a person whose life has meaning because I am connected to and care about many things larger than

myself. If I did not tithe, I would lose track of these truths about who I am.

Work devoted to something greater than yourself lifts you out of the narrow sphere of individual concerns, enlarges your perspective, and provides context for the joys and concerns of your own life. It's a reality check, bringing us constantly back to the truth of our seventh Principle, in which we affirm the interconnected web of all existence. No lay leader gets to act alone. It means working for and with a group of people who have intertwining needs, hopes, fears, and expectations, all to help fulfill a common mission that binds them together. What better opportunity to learn over and over again that we are mutually interdependent? Lay service means claiming your own strand of the interdependent web while honoring the needs of others. It means being a firsthand witness to the power of diversity united in a single mission.

There is yet another level which opens up most fully when you see service to your congregation as a spiritual practice, when you look at leadership through a spiritual lens. As the following chapters will make clear, leadership can provide countless opportunities to learn more about yourself—your strengths and challenges—and how you work with others. You will have the chance to practice patience and learn about listening, really listening, to people with whom you disagree yet who may well have something you need to hear. These are valuable lessons. And they are only the beginning.

Kyoto, Japan, is home to a number of Zen monasteries. One of them has a beautiful zendo, the meditation hall where the monks gather for their meditation. Outside, an icy mountain stream cascades down in a beautiful waterfall, at the base of which lies a large flat rock. The senior monks do their zazen, or meditation practice, here, beneath the icy water, rather than in the zendo. Anyone can meditate in the quiet of the meditation hall; it takes sincere concentration to meditate with a distraction such as this. It might seem easier to separate your prayer time from your productive time, your spirituality from the rest of your life, but it doesn't work like that. All the great spiritual traditions teach that life is ultimately One, that there is no separation possible, and that we must be able to find our calm in the midst of confusion, our peace in the heart of our problems, our spirituality in the center of everything else.

In other words, your lay leadership can't truly be a spiritual practice if you consider its spiritual dimension only as a set of fringe benefits. The challenge is to radically re-conceptualize the very purpose of lay leadership, not from the congregation's perspective but from your own. Selfless giving is undoubtedly a spiritual virtue, but if that comes to dominate your involvement in church life, then that community will become for you a place of work and pressure, no longer your true spiritual home. Imagine how your work for the congregation might be transformed if you approached it primarily as your spiritual practice, and secondarily as helping the church fulfill its mission. If this sounds too selfish, keep reading. You may find that this approach will actually make you a more effective leader. Think of your time and energy as congregational resources, and yourself as a responsible steward of those resources. A key aspect of that stewardship is to avoid burnout, so tailoring your lay leadership so that it truly grows your soul is essential.

Many spiritual traditions emphasize that the accomplishment of a task is secondary to the experience of doing the task. This is one way of understanding the concept of nonattachment to outcomes—whether or not a thing gets done is far less important than how one attempts to do it. Is your mind focused or distracted? Is your intention clear or dissipated? Do you experience joy or resentment while doing it? We've all heard the saying, "What matters is not whether you win or lose, but how you play the game." Many people today understand this as a cynical cliché used to calm pre-game jitters or soothe the wounded psyches of those who lost. Few people really believe it. We know—because we are reminded in countless ways both subtle and overt—that winning really does matter. Some people go so far as to say it's the *only* thing that matters and, in fact, how you play is of no real consequence at all. (As long as you win, that is.)

Accomplishment and productivity matter greatly in our capitalist culture. Setting goals and accomplishing them is tremendously important. As congregations have adopted the language of business, and boards are striving to be better managers, we've been told again and again about the necessity of setting goals that are "SMART"—specific, measurable, attainable, realistic, and timely.

Yet every spiritual tradition humanity has ever devised teaches the same lesson—that how we do what we do matters far more than what we do. The secret of life, we're told, is that it is the journey itself that matters and not the arrival at the destination. The person who gives little with a pure heart does "more good" than the one who gives much in order to show off. If you do the "right thing" for the "wrong reason" you receive no merit. Again and again, in different ways, humanity's spiritual traditions encourage us to focus on the experience of the doing and not the product of our actions.

Two different ways of looking at the world—the way of the world and the way of the world's religions. What if the world's religions are right? What if it really *doesn't* matter whether you win or lose? What if the most important thing *is* how you play the game? Then it is possible that it doesn't really matter whether you get through the agenda in record time if, to do so, you must ignore your congregation's commitment to inclusiveness and shut people down so you can be more efficient. It is possible that it doesn't really matter whether you decide that thorny issue tonight, that what really matters is the quality of your discussion. It is possible that it doesn't even matter if you make your stewardship goal and fully fund your budget, that what really matters is the heart and faith and generosity that went into the effort.

For some, this is a new—and possibly even heretical—way of looking at things. If the church were a business, of course, efficiency, productivity, and the bottom line really would matter. Perhaps the most important thing to a small business, even a non-profit, is to accomplish the goals of the organization as effectively and efficiently as possible. Completion of tasks matters. Balanced budgets matter. Success, however that's defined, most definitely matters.

But churches are not small businesses, even though they often act that way. They are not even typical non-profits because they are, first and foremost, communities. They strive to embody the ideals represented by the familiar term *beloved community*. South African Archbishop Desmond Tutu once said that the church should be "an audiovisual aid for the sake of the world," showing how the world should be. And so here, despite the many similarities with traditional businesses, different rules apply. There is, so to speak, a new bottom line and the measure of success is entirely different.

Self-Discovery

At the Temple of Apollo at Delphi—where a priestess served as oracle of that god—pilgrims would pause in the forecourt to ponder the inscription *gnothi seauton*, "Know thyself." Before you can hear the message of the gods, it seems to have been saying, you must know who and what you are. Good advice for us today.

One of the first ways that congregational leadership can serve you as a spiritual practice—and one of the tools for transforming it from a mere job into a fulfilling spiritual practice—is to take advantage of opportunities for leadership to teach you about yourself. After all, at some level, aren't all spiritual practices pathways of self-discovery? Lay leadership is no different.

You can begin by asking yourself, How do I understand the word *leader*? This is a sticking point for many people in congregations today. They may see themselves as a committee member or as a person involved with some project or program, they may even be the chair of this or that task group, but still not consider themselves a leader. This is a problem and explains why many calls for "new leaders" often go unanswered.

Some distrust the term *leadership*—leaders are people who tell everybody else what to do and how to do it. Leaders exercise "power over" and are relics of a patriarchal system that is no longer appropriate in the twenty-first century (if, indeed, it ever was). We prefer collaboration and consensus. Leader? I would never want to be one of those.

For others, the term *leader* is held in too high esteem—leaders are people like Martin Luther King Jr. or Dorothy Dix, who bravely stood out in front of the crowd and showed people the way. Leaders have the "vision thing" and can inspire legions of followers. Leader? I could never be one of those.

Think of people in your own congregation—perhaps you are one—who have been in charge of this project or that program for years yet who, if they ever heard themselves described as one of the "church leaders," would strongly demur. Everyone knows that if you want to get something done you should go ask Dawn or Alice or Ken, but if you invited them to a meeting of church leaders they'd most likely politely decline. They'd say that there are other people who are smarter, or better in meetings, are younger, or older, or something or other that makes them more of a leader. And yet, time and again, church members go to the Dawns and Alices and Bobs when they want to know how to get something done. Who, then, is really leading whom?

Leadership is both more and less than either extreme. The analogy is sometimes made to geese which, during their transcontinental flights assume a "V" formation. The goose out front is quite clearly the leader, not only helping to show the way but taking on the task of breaking through the headwinds to make it easier for all those who follow. Yet the updraft of all the beating wings of the "followers" makes the leader's flight easier. And it's also true that, at regular intervals, the leader drops back into a follower's position and another leader comes to the front. Shared leadership is not an oxymoron, and the true place of a leader is neither as high nor low as it is sometimes set.

Yet if the term *leader* still carries too much baggage, use another one. Here are some suggestions: *facilitator, convener, point person, servant.* This last one might surprise you, yet the notion of the "servant leader" is quite well known in many religious traditions—the one who leads in service to the wider community, not for her or his own good alone. The term *minister* itself—etymologically as well as theologically—means "one who serves." This, one might argue, is the quintessential understanding of leadership in the religious context, and it can go far in helping to free the term *leader* from some of the unnecessary, and unhelpful, weight it too often carries.

This is an especially appropriate understanding of leadership in communities like Unitarian Universalist congregations which, because of their congregational polity, reserve ultimate authority for the gathered community. Leaders have only the authority given to them by their communities—in the end it is the church as a whole which directs its own course. Leaders are but servants of the wider community. So isn't it easy to see how this

understanding of leadership lends itself to opportunities for developing spiritual virtues such as discernment,
patience, courage, and humility?

After looking at how you understand the word *leader*,
you can then consider how you understand yourself as a
leader. What kind are you? There are a great many ways
to be a leader. Knowing the kind of leader you are—
sometimes called your leadership style or temperament
—can help reduce the feelings of frustration that come
up when different styles collide. This also goes to show
that church leadership really is a spiritual practice. Even
before you begin you're given an opportunity to look
deeply at who and how you are when dealing with
others—these could be fellow committee members, of
course, but also your family (immediate or extended),
co-workers, strangers on the street, God. This is about so
much more than how to be a good Board member!

Back in the 1970s you might have been expected to
know your zodiac sign; today you're more apt to be asked
your Myers-Briggs type, yet the point is essentially the
same—there are myriad ways for people to categorize
and classify themselves. *Leadership style*, *organizational
temperament*, and *personality type* are just three of the current phrases used to help people discover more about
why they're good at the things they're good at, why they
like the things they like—and why they're not and don't.
There are many other models too, of course, including
the plethora of silly "tests" on Facebook, such as, Which
Harry Potter character are you? Which Catholic saint are

you? or Which Beatles song are you? Each of these models creates a series of metaphoric descriptions you can use to better understand yourself.

Even the superficial kinds of tests can have merit if they open a window onto three fundamental questions: Who are you? Who are you in relation to the task(s) you're doing? and Who are you in relation to the people with whom you are working? Knowing your type can help you to know how you prefer to approach different kinds of tasks on your church's Board, for instance, or even whether you'd prefer to serve your church as a Board member or a member of the worship team. It can also help you understand how you relate with others.

For instance, someone who gets energy from solitary pursuits may need to be sure to schedule some downtime during leadership retreats, because she will need to recharge her batteries. Someone else may need to be patient in meetings with the Board member who tends to be more focused on facts than feelings. Getting an idea of who you are and how you operate—and who the people you work with are—can help in all sorts of ways from self-care to interpersonal relations.

As you engage your work in the church with your "spiritual lens" on you will notice a myriad of opportunities to ask questions about yourself: Why was that task particularly attractive to me? Why was this other thing so difficult? Why does this person always seem to rub me the wrong way? Why do I almost always seem to agree with this other person? Taking each of these as a kind of koan, a profound riddle with which to wrestle or dance, will do much toward revealing your depths to yourself.

If you begin with an understanding of your personality type—for example, a Myers-Briggs type—you will have a framework in which to carry on this internal investigation. For this reason, some congregations have instituted a practice of having each new "crop" of leaders take a Myers-Briggs test during their annual leadership retreat, and some committee chairs do it less formally with their committees when the church as a whole hasn't taken on such an approach. Sometimes this is a major program of the leadership development team, offering leadership styles inventories several times throughout the year as part of the congregation's adult education programming.

As you get to know more about yourself, you may see areas in which you need strength and support. A popular trend in the 1990s was to wear bracelets with the letters *W-W-J-D?*, standing for What Would Jesus Do? The idea was that someone trying to live a truly Christian life could benefit from asking himself on a regular basis what Jesus would do in any given circumstance—doing so would take him out of his own ego needs and allow his "higher self" to act. In some ways this is analogous to the television character George Costanza from *Seinfeld* deciding to do the opposite of whatever his initial inclination was, since his life was a failure when he followed his own leanings. Both of these practices are based on the notion that we are not required to follow our initial impulses and that, in fact, doing so is often *not* in our best interest.

Yet not everyone will see the efficacy of asking whether Jesus would allow the church to be rented by a day care program, or whether to move from cookies and cake to veggies and fruit at the kids' snack table during coffee hour. And not everyone feels as negatively about themselves as George in *Seinfeld*. Yet many of us do have what might be called a "leadership saint," someone whose leadership we've found to be inspirational. Perhaps it's Martin Luther King Jr. organizing the Montgomery bus boycott, or Mohandas Gandhi leading the Salt March. Maybe it's the Berrigan brothers standing courageously against the war in Vietnam. Maybe it's Mother Jones, with her strength of will, or your own mother in the way she ran your household. Perhaps you have never identified anyone in this way, but more than likely there is someone you have known or just heard of who embodies all that you think about when you hear the word *leader*.

In traditional Catholicism, one of the roles of the saints is to provide examples to emulate—and many people grew up knowing the stories of the saints as well as any of the stories in the Bible itself. People would often find a "patron saint," one whose example particularly spoke to them and gave them courage or hope. This is not a form of unconscious polytheism—with a different saint (god) for different spheres of life—nor is it simply an example of magical thinking whereby one can pray to the appropriate saint for the desired outcome. (Although both of these are sometimes present in the way devotion to the saints is played out.) Rather, at its root, the adoration of the saints is aimed at offering role models of the holy life. So instead of asking only, What would Jesus do? one could also ask, What would Francis do? or, What would Theresa do? And those who really know the lives of the saints could look to the saint who might most be able to provide a useful example.

Perhaps you could identify a leadership saint or two. It need not be someone religious or spiritual. A leader from a secular field who personifies leadership qualities that you wish to emulate will work just as well, perhaps even better. It might not even be someone generally recognized as a leader but someone who embodies an insight and wisdom you find powerful.

Once you've identified your "saints," find out all you can about them. Look them up online. Read any biographies (or autobiographies) you can. Learn the stories of their lives well enough that you can call on their example when you need a sense of guidance.

You might want to find a picture and put it in a special place in your home or office so that throughout your day you could bring your leadership saint to mind. You could download a digital image to your computer to use as a desktop background or as a screen saver. You could even carry a picture of them in your PDA or your cell phone so that, during a difficult meeting, you could call them clearly to mind and ask yourself, What would she or he do in this situation? None of this is to suggest that you should slavishly adhere to what you think Tony Robbins or Aung San Suu Kyi would do in any given situation. Instead, this practice provides an opportunity to consider your own impulses and instincts from a different point of view. And a considered opinion is almost always preferable to a knee-jerk response.

One reason for the Catholic practice of learning about the lives of the saints is the assumption that as we learn more about them, as we spend time with them so to speak, we find ourselves taking on more of their qualities. The same assumption is the basis of this leadership saint practice and, it should be noted, the same assumption underlies the field of personality theory.

It's important to recognize that one's personality type is not something that is carved in stone. Carl Jung, arguably the grandfather of personality type theory, believed that people moved through the different types in different situations and in different stages of their lives. And as you learn more about the types, and associate with people who personify them, you will naturally strengthen some of your weaker areas or venture into arenas that you might currently shy away from.

For this reason, if no other, it is essential to recognize that no one type is "better" than another. This is so important—and so often misunderstood. Each type has its own strengths and weaknesses; each has its own challenges and presents its own benefits. Quite often people feel that "the grass is always greener" about personality types—introverts wish they were extroverts and, perhaps only surprising to the introverts, vice versa. Yet the Delphi oracle implied that wisdom is to be found in knowing yourself, not wishing to be someone else.

Knowing your type helps you understand why certain things come easily for you while other things are a challenge, why you seem naturally drawn to certain kinds of tasks and situations and tend to stay away from others, why you naturally seem to align with certain kinds of people and find others confusing. And from that comes a kind of power, an ease. The language of personality type provides a way of seeing yourself that gives you permission to acknowledge strengths and weaknesses and let go of the belief that you ought to be able to have it all and do it all. This can be a tremendous asset as you prepare for your role in church leadership—and it can be one of the gifts you receive as part of your service to the church.

No Is as Sacred as Yes

If there's one major barrier to the idea of lay leadership as a spiritual practice, it's that, in far too many of our congregations, only a handful of people do the vast majority of the work. This is sometimes referred to as the 80/20 rule—the oft-repeated statistic that 80 percent of the work is done by 20 percent of the people. Over time, those doing the work not only tend to stay a consistent proportion of the whole but also are likely to remain *the same people*. Sometimes these stalwarts stay in the same positions year after year, sometimes they rotate seemingly endlessly through the various leadership roles of the congregation, but in too many congregations today a small group does most of the work and has been doing so for far too long.

These church leaders are tired of always being the ones to step up and pitch in, tired of asking for help with no one coming forward, tired of doing all the work and having all the responsibility. They ask, Isn't this supposed to be my spiritual home? Then they (finally) step down from all the leadership roles they've been holding and, all too frequently, leave the church altogether.

Meanwhile, there are inevitably those among the other 80 percent who want to feel more closely connected to their spiritual community, to contribute to it in a tangible way, but feel that there's no place at the table for them. The first problem these folks face is that they are overwhelmed. The people who seem to have been stuck doing everything have not only been getting the work done but have also been modeling, inadvertently, a particular understanding of leadership—that leadership in the church means doing everything. This can make it extremely difficult for the person who wants to do simply *something* to step up. The majority of congregations don't have very many examples of people doing something, while other people do other things. Rather, we often see the same people doing everything, forever, and then burning out. (Not exactly a great strategy for recruiting new leaders!) So a lot of these 80 percent folks don't step up because they just can't imagine doing everything that Jane, Dorothy, or Tavia has been doing all these years. They don't want to burn out in their church—they want to be lit up!

In a healthy congregation there are generally two kinds of work for lay leaders—committee work and hands-on tasks. Unfortunately, these two are often conflated, and the committees are made up of worker bees who do all of the work of the church. The Religious Education Committee is comprised of the most committed teachers; the Buildings and Grounds Committee are the ones who show up for the Spring Clean-up Event; the

Fellowship (or Fun!) Committee hosts all of the Congregational Game Nights.

Even though many of our congregations have been operating this way since time immemorial, the model is problematic. Committee work is quite separate and distinct from hands-on work and vice versa. Each requires different skills, temperaments, and personality types. Lack of clarity about the kind of work that is involved can lead to several difficulties. It can be hard to get people to step up if they're unsure or misinformed about what is required of them. Leaders can burn out easily or, at the least, get discouraged when they think they've signed on for one thing only to find themselves doing something else. And important work can get left undone if one group tries to do everything. One of the reasons for finding out your leadership style is to help you discern the kinds of roles that best suit your skills, interests, and "type." Also, it helps the congregation to remember that there are both different leadership types and different leadership roles.

Have you ever sat through a meeting with someone who was obviously itching to stop all of the processing and discussing and just to get down to *doing something*? You could see his frustration building. Or maybe you have participated in a project with someone who wanted to talk through each and every step. As problematic as these people and their behavior may have seemed at the time—or as difficult as everyone else's behavior may have seemed to them at the time—they were doing nothing inherently wrong. They were simply in the wrong place at the wrong time.

In general, the purpose of a committee is to coordinate and celebrate. So ideally the Fun Committee would decide that each month there should be some kind of fun congregational event—a Chinese dinner in February, a family game night in March, a talent show in April. Or perhaps it wouldn't even get this specific and they would decide only that there should be some family-friendly activity each month. The committee would then find individuals in the congregation with a knack for organizing who were looking for some way to get involved without serving on a committee and would sign them up to host just one of these activities. Committee members would coordinate, strategize, plan—all the kinds of processing work committees are meant to do—and the host for each event would actually put on their own particular event. In other words, the committee would plan the big picture and the worker would focus on the details of carrying it out (including what you could think of as the "administrative support" of the committee). Then, when things came to an end, the committee would celebrate the work of the hosts (because it's always important to "pay" your volunteers!).

Interestingly, the same 80/20 ratio shows up here as earlier. (In fact, the 80/20 split shows up so often in organizations that in management theory it has a name—"Pareto's Principle.") Roughly 80 percent of people report that they're interested in doing something to help their congregation but don't want to serve on a committee, while 20 percent say that they're really interested in doing the kind of work that committees are supposed to do. Meanwhile, committee work, when understood in this way, would take up about 20 percent of the energy of a congregation while the hands-on work that's needed would use about 80 percent. So the problem in most congregations isn't really a lack of volunteer energy, as is so often assumed. It's more of a distribution issue. And even that can be attributed to misunderstanding where the energy is needed. This is why this same dynamic can be seen in large multi-staff congregations and small lay-led fellowships.

Does your congregation have a listing of the committees, task forces, working groups, etc., with which you might get involved? If not, go through the church's newsletter and calendar, jotting down all of the meetings and events to create such a list. Then, next to each one, note whether it seems to be a committee (i.e., coordinating and celebrating) or a hands-on working group. For many of our congregations it is both. Note which one you think it *should* be. Next to this, make a notation of the skill set, personality type, and/or leadership style that you think is most needed for each. (Remember that many tasks call for more than one.) Then circle the ones that seem right for you based on what you've learned about yourself. Does anything surprise you?

So now that you know yourself as you do, where do you want to spend your time and energy? How can your talents best serve your congregation? These are questions that often go unasked because the needs of our congregations can seem so overwhelming that, to put it bluntly, it often seems that they just need a warm body and those of us willing to answer the call go where we're told we're needed. Questions such as, What do I *want* to do? and Where might I best be of use? also aren't considered because of the way our churches often ask for help.

Bill is a devoted member of the congregation, and when he hears that they're having trouble finding a treasurer he volunteers, even though he's not really a detail kind of guy. But somebody's got to step up to the plate, right? What follows is two years of frustration on everybody's part. Or Donna, who's a member of the Board and the chair of the Adult Programs Committee and the only person on the Building and Grounds Committee, signs on to head up the Spring Auction so that this important fundraiser won't go without leadership. At the end of the year she decides to step away from all her church work and even stops attending services. She says she needs a "break." Have you ever heard about—or experienced—stories like these?

Yet if our service to the church is to be a spiritual practice, and not just a road to resentment, then it is worth taking the time to practice the ancient art of discernment. Many congregations have begun to move from Nominating Committees—whose charge, essentially, is to fill slots on a roster—to Leadership Development Councils—which help develop the leadership potential of the membership. The assumption is that, as members develop into leaders, they will naturally find their places within the church's structure and will do so more organically, with less pressure on the front end and less burn out on the back end.

Some congregations have even begun to encourage their members to say "no" when asked. After all, one of the leading causes of leadership burnout is the syndrome known as "taking on too much." How many times have you taken on some task when you've really known you shouldn't? Someone has to do it, after all, and you know that you *can*. And since no one else is stepping up . . . .

But what if, during the membership orientation, you heard the idea that in this congregation "your *no* is as sacred as your *yes*," that here you were expected to say "yes" only when you could say it with an open heart and a clear conscience? And that you were expected to say "no" as often as that felt like the right thing to say?

In this congregation Bill doesn't step up to become Treasurer—a role for which he really isn't suited—and Donna doesn't take on that one task too many. Both of them say "no," even though the need of the congregation is real. They both know that they are not responsible for everything by themselves, that the whole congregation is responsible for itself and that they can only do what they can do. As the great Unitarian minister Edward Everett Hale said, "I am only one, but still I am one. I cannot do everything, but still I can do something. And because I cannot do everything I will not refuse to do the something that I can do." Bill and Donna know that part of making leadership into a spiritual practice is discerning what that *something* is.

Because he didn't step up to become Treasurer, Bill is available when he hears about the need for someone to head up the Spring Auction. He knows that details aren't his strong suit, but that he's great at talking with people so he'd be good at getting items donated. And since he's a natural ham, he'd make a great auctioneer. He volunteers to do those things as co-leader. And Donna, who because of her years of experience knows just about everyone in the congregation, knows that there's a relatively new member who's hesitant to take on a leadership role, yet who might be willing to co-lead with Bill. And since this person *is* detail-oriented, yet kind of shy, the two would complement each other perfectly.

And what of the hard-to-fill Treasurer's position? It remains unfilled for half the church year. The Finance Committee takes on some extra duties, with the collaborative supervision of the Board, and the two bodies have some worthwhile conversations about why apparently no one wants this job. They re-write the job description to make the position more manageable, recognize the need for some part-time paid bookkeeping assistance, and by mid-year so reorder things that they now have several people interested in taking on the new role. They also have had the chance to wrestle with who they are as an organization and who they want to be.

It is actually better for your congregation in the long run if people don't sign up reluctantly and with resentment just to keep a program afloat. This might seem heretical, but the church's Spring Fair was made for the congregation, not the congregation for the fair. The worst thing that could happen is that nobody signs up to lead the fair. The budget may become a little tight(er) but you'll also have learned a valuable lesson: apparently no one is invested in this program anymore.

Our congregations often keep many things afloat primarily because they always have. A truly alive congregation, one that is really focused on deepening the spiritual lives of its members and making a real difference in the world, will become quite practiced in holding memorial services for programs. Few things pass the test of time—that's why it's a test—yet our congregations spend a tremendous amount of energy and talent (and money) keeping programs and projects on life support. In the process they virtually guarantee the burnout of the volunteers who step up yet again to save the day.

So it actually benefits everyone for leaders—and potential leaders—to take a moment to ask whether they really want to take on the position they're considering: Does it fit with my current interests? Does it mesh with my skill sets, my personality type, and my leadership style? Do I actually have the time to do it? The church always has needs—and these needs are, indeed, real—yet saying "yes" is not always the best way to serve those needs. At least not without spending some time in good old-fashioned discernment first.

Ask yourself some questions when faced with a possible new position or task: What are the things I'm already committed to? What are the things I'd like to be doing (for myself, for my family) for which I currently don't seem to have the time? What are the things I'm doing now that are really just a waste of time and not as important as other things I'm doing or would like to do? After this kind of self-examination you're ready to sit in a Council meeting and keep your hands on the table when the request goes out for the chair of a new working group on governance.

While you're looking at the time you have, you can also analyze your interest: Do I like tasks that require interaction and collaboration with others? Would I rather sit in front of the computer at home after the kids go to sleep sending out emails or searching for information on the web? Do I like one-time-only events or ongoing activities? When you know these things about yourself you will be in a much better position to take on only those tasks that really capture your imagination, speak to your soul, and for which you have time.

This one practice of people taking an inventory of their likes and availability, if implemented widely, can cut down leadership burnout in congregations by a tremendous amount. You don't *have* to sign up for tasks you find uninteresting or burdensome, even if that's been the culture of your congregation to date. Your Board or committee may need to learn how to broaden the reach of its asking, and find new ways to frame tasks to help people see their value, but if the thing is important it has to be important to someone. That someone doesn't have to be you.

As Howard Thurman once said, "Don't ask what the world needs. Ask what makes you come alive, and then do that thing. Because what the world needs is people who are alive." The same goes for our congregations.

Mindful Meetings

Whether you're the Board President or a teacher's aid on Sunday morning, chances are that some part of your leadership will involve meetings. You may plan them or attend them, but they will be part of your experience. If you're like most people, the word *meeting* evokes an image of a poorly lit room with stale air and uncomfortable chairs, a meandering conversation and wandering attention. But it doesn't have to be that way.

If you've ever seen a Japanese tea ceremony, perhaps the quintessence of spiritual rituals, it is certainly not pulled together at the last minute and there is no detail too small to be considered. The way the room is arranged, the guests greeted, the implements brought into the room and laid out—all of it is meticulously and mindfully undertaken as part of the ceremony itself. Can you envision your meetings handled this way? All it would take is some focused attention, starting with the agenda.

An agenda provides a tool that can help you keep the spirituality of your service in the forefront of your thinking. At a convenient time a day or so before the meeting—not too far in advance, when you'll likely forget what you've done, nor too near, when you might be rushed—take out the agenda and look at it carefully. Visualize the people who will be with you around the table, and any interactions you all might have had already regarding any of the agenda items (the old business). Think about what you might know about the feelings likely to be in the room regarding any new business. Hear the conversations. Who might bring up what objections? What "hot buttons" do you see?

While you're imagining the meeting, check in with yourself. How do you feel? Does anything you've envisioned make you feel anxious? Excited? Challenged? Disinterested? Do you notice any feelings in your body, such as a tightness in your shoulders and jaw or a roiling in your belly? Maybe you feel a lightness in your forehead and an enlivening uptick in your heartbeat.

Discovering how you feel while thinking about the upcoming meeting can have tremendous benefits. For one thing, it can help prepare you so that, in the actual meeting, you *respond* more than *react*. Sitting meditatively, prayerfully, with the agenda beforehand can help you bring a mindful consciousness to the meeting so that you can deal with the issues in front of you rather than projecting onto them all of your past associations and future hopes and fears. What is it like to be with *this* group of people working on *this* budget in *this* congregational and cultural climate? What are the questions and opportunities raised by *this* proposal in light of the larger spirit and mission of the church?

Very often our reactions are colored by so much that has nothing to do with the issue at hand—our feelings about the person who's making the proposal, for instance, or the kind of day we had at work, might lead us to argue against something that, on another day from someone else, we might actually support. Or we might be anticipating a certain reaction from someone else—a negative pattern, perhaps, that we feel sure will repeat itself—and launch a pre-emptive strike that, more often than not, leads to the very kind of confrontation we had hoped to avoid.

Such things are largely unconscious and quite understandable—this is how most people behave most of the time. Meditating on the agenda can help prepare you for your own unconscious reactions—since it's all happening in your imagination, you can be sure that whatever comes up is the unconscious stuff you'd otherwise be bringing to the table. Rehearsing, as it were, gives you the opportunity to see it in advance and, perhaps, make more conscious choices.

We don't have any power over how others act, yet we do have quite a bit of control over our own actions, *if we become conscious*! Meetings might still get heated, convoluted, or self-indulgent, but the practice of using the agenda as a prayer book will allow you, as Rudyard Kipling put it, to "keep your head while all about you are losing theirs." And it can help you to engage the work of the meeting from the perspective of your highest, deepest, and most aware self. Imagine never again leaving the church and saying in your car what you wish you'd said in the meeting!

This could also be a place to bring your leadership saint to bear. Looking at the meeting to come, which of your saints might you want to bring with you? Whose insights and spirit would you especially like to have at the table with you? This is another way to prepare for the meeting to come—and have you ever noticed how many spiritual practices involve a period of conscious and intentional preparation?

There is nothing inherently more spiritual about the top of a mountain than the cigar shop on the corner. There are many suitable places in the church where your group could meet. Yet if you want to deepen the spiritual quality of your work together, it makes sense to pay attention to the quality of your meeting space. Consider the pages and pages taken up in the Hebrew Scriptures describing the furnishings of the temple or ponder the simple elegance of a Zen temple—both express an attention to the quality of one's surroundings.

Think about which room in the church will be most conducive to your purposes. If it's a long meeting, consider a room with comfortable seating, good lighting, and adequate ventilation. Have someone get there early and straighten up the room so that it's not cluttered—distraction in the outer space will lead to distractions in your inner space as well. If you're using a table, put a chalice and perhaps a flower in the middle. You might set out several large-print copies of the church's (or your group's) mission statement so people can see them easily.

Some people think it is better to have meetings in people's homes and in some instances, and for some purposes, this is true. However, most of the time it is better to meet at the church if possible. People who are new to the congregation may feel less intimidated about going to the church than to the house of another member they may not know well, and meetings at the church reconnect people to the congregation itself. There's also the added benefit that a congregation that has a busy building with the lights on and the rooms filled just *feels* more alive and exciting—both to members and to prospective members in the wider community.

Thinking about the church building as your "church home" and taking care of it that way is tremendously important. Fostering a feeling of shared ownership and shared responsibility for our facilities is a key issue, not only for Unitarian Universalists but for many other religious communities as well. People today often treat their public buildings as if they are there to be used but will be cared for by somebody else. A congregation that takes care of its building—that treats even its meeting rooms as if they are sanctuaries, which, of course, they are—will find that in no time there is a dramatic change in the spirit of the community as a whole. And it can begin with your meeting.

Many congregations, inspired by such things as lay leadership schools and the cross-fertilization that occurs as people move from congregation to congregation, have begun to add elements such as a chalice lighting or a check-in to their regular meeting agendas. Yet far too many congregations do these things by rote without really thinking about *why* they do them. This can lead to the oft-asked question, Do we really need to do a check-in tonight? You need not adopt all of these elements, yet each fills its own purpose, and like the separate elements of a worship service, they do add up to more together than the sum of their parts. Still, if you feel the need to begin with some rather than all, start with those that feed the most unmet needs of your group. Here is a little explanation of why such elements can serve deep purposes:

Opening Words: Just as when we gather for worship, we gather for our meetings from different places (literally and metaphorically) and opening words help us to come together as one group. They give our minds and our hearts something to consider, and remind us of the deeper context in which we will do the work we have come together to do. Opening words can also help us get to know one another better, if different people choose the readings and select passages that truly speak to them.

Chalice Lighting: Lighting a chalice at the beginning of a meeting is a ritual reminder that the work of the Finance Committee, for instance, is not separate from the work of a Sunday morning. For all the reasons we light the flame at the latter it is good to light it at the former as well.

Check-in: There is a real human need to connect, and rest assured people will do it one way or another. The cynic will say that if you do not provide a formal time at the beginning of the meeting for people to check in they will be checking in informally throughout the meeting! Less cynically, though, this time is a way of demonstrating to one another that we affirm each other's worth and dignity as individuals. It's a way of asking, Who is in the room today? What has been happening in your life? What's on your mind and in your heart that affects who you are right now? This not only helps each individual to be fully present, it can help the group function more coherently.

Vibes-Watcher: Quite common on the national scene, not yet so frequent at the level of local congregations, many meetings designate one person to observe the "tone" of the meeting. Are things getting heated? Is everyone being heard? Is anyone being shut down or shut out? Are we forgetting anything we've said was important for us to remember? Having such a person does not absolve everyone from paying attention, but it does ensure that *someone* is. In some groups this person is charged with speaking up throughout the meeting; other groups ask for feedback during the checkout. However your group chooses to make use of a "vibes-watcher," such a person provides a way of taking seriously your commitments to doing things more consciously.

Breath Breaks: When a meeting gets heated it can be a great benefit to take a moment to gather yourselves by taking two or three centering breaths. Some groups have a policy in which any member can ask the group as a whole to stop their deliberations wherever they are and breathe together. All discussion then immediately stops and everyone breathes in and out for an agreed upon amount of time—three to five breaths, for instance, or for one minute—and then the conversation resumes where it left off. No conversation is needed about this "breath break," this spiritual "time out." There is no discussion, no explanation needed, no vote taken. It is enough that someone feels the need for it—and nothing is then said afterward. The practice simply gives everyone a chance to literally catch their breath and regain their composure.

Check-out: Setting aside five or ten minutes at the end of a meeting to process how the meeting went may seem like a luxury, yet those who do so often report that it has made their meetings more efficient and so they find they have the time. A check-out is a time for people to make a brief statement about how the meeting felt and, as noted above, it can be a time for the vibes-watcher to offer her observations.

How you do what you do matters. These practices can affect the quality of the time you spend doing your business and so are just as important as the business itself. In fact, many congregations find that when these activities are truly attended to the meetings go so much more smoothly that they actually take less time than before, even though there is now all of this "extra" stuff.

Just as looking mindfully ahead at the meeting to come can be a way of centering yourself in the spirit of your service, so looking backward at the past meeting by meditating on the minutes can have a similar effect. Ideally, your committee or task group will produce useful minutes—ones that not only provide an institutional record of who was present, what was discussed, what decisions were made, and what next steps were generated, but also that convey something of the "spirit" of the meeting. That way, someone who was not present could have a sense of what it felt like to be there. These kinds of minutes are both institutionally and spiritually useful.

Assuming that your committee or task group produces useful minutes in a timely manner, take some time prior to your next meeting to look them over in the same meditative, prayerful way you've engaged with the upcoming agenda. Except with this practice you'll be remembering rather than imagining. Ask yourself these kinds of questions: How do you feel about how you behaved? About the group's interactions? Do you think the group broke faith with one another, or with your congregation at any point? Do you wish that one of your leadership saints had been there?

Looking back, do you see that anyone was silenced or shut out? Did anyone dominate the rest? Was anyone forgotten—both those in the meeting room with you and those in the wider congregation? Gandhi once said that he tried to imagine the impact his decisions would have on the poorest man or woman he could think of. Did your Board or task force consider the marginalized in your congregation (or your community, or our world) while doing its work? Did you keep faith with the spirit of your congregation and its understanding of its mission? Was it a *religious* meeting?

This might be a new way of thinking about your work. In many of the Christian traditions there is a well-known song with the refrain, "They'll know we are Christians by our love." In other words, as Christians, they will behave in such a way that the love they show one another—and everyone they meet—will be an advertisement of their Christianity. As Dom Hélder Pessoa Câmara famously said, "Be careful how you live your life for it is the only Gospel others will read."

So was the last meeting of your Board or working group a demonstration of your congregation's understanding of itself as a faith community? If your meeting had been videotaped and televised, would it have been a good example of what being a Unitarian Universalist is all about? Would others have been able to look at it and recognize you unmistakably as who you are? Would you have wanted to include it in your marketing video for your congregation as an example of what your church is really like?

Having reflected back on the past meeting, is there anything that needs to be brought up again? Are there any apologies that need to be made? Commendations offered? Most importantly, is there anything that you, yourself, would like to do differently during this coming meeting? Reflecting deeply on our behavior—individually and as a group—is a sure way of moving us from being merely reactive to the business at hand to being responsive to the spirit of the moment.

As noted earlier, seeing leadership as an opportunity and a tool for spiritual growth also means seeing the work of leadership in a new light. Accomplishing tasks becomes secondary; learning to engage deeply and mindfully with yourself and others while looking at your group's work in light of the spirit of your congregation becomes primary. So there may be a lot of work (tasks) to do, yet if there is work (engagement) left undone it behooves you all to set the former aside to continue to dance with the latter.

If everyone on the committee or task force covenants with one another to do this, it will go a long way toward helping the group as a whole stay focused on the spiritual dimensions of the work. Likewise, beginning your meeting with the church's or committee's mission statement, and keeping them physically in front of you throughout the meeting will also help you to keep from straying too far from that clear focus. And, as mentioned, a vibes-watcher can be invaluable. (Even more helpful is the understanding that everyone internally assumes the role of vibes-watcher.)

If the quality of the discussion is more important than the quantity of the decisions, you will likely find yourselves encountering some issues about which you're unable to come to a clear decision. That, then, *is* your decision for now. "We don't know," is, in fact, an answer, even though it's rarely given by leaders. (And how many terrible problems might have been averted if our leaders had said "I don't know"instead of manufacturing assurance they didn't possess!) In communities that use consensus for decision making it is considered perfectly appropriate to allow a deliberation to continue until a decision emerges rather than to prematurely force a conclusion to the discussion.

It has been said that one of the worst punishments in hell is spending eternity scheduling meetings! Yet just as important as the physical space for a meeting is the space in time in which it occurs. There are a myriad of practical matters to consider. When is the room you want available? What is an optimal time to discuss the issue at hand? When are the participants available? There are no hard and fast rules that apply to every situation except, perhaps, this one: *Do as much as you can to be as fair as you can and then be as forgiving as you can when it doesn't work perfectly.*

Still, there are some general guidelines that may help you keep in mind the spiritual aspect of your meetings while you juggle the practical aspects of the scheduling. Generally speaking, a spiritual practice needs to be engaged with regularly and with some frequency for maximum effectiveness. It's the same with any other practice—if you pick up a musical instrument, a paintbrush, or your tap shoes only every other month or so, you will make progress but it will be slow going. Considering people's busy schedules, regular monthly meetings make good sense. If there's more work to be done, meet more regularly, but less often than monthly will make it hard to do much more than transact business. Irregularly scheduled meetings do not develop any kind of rhythm, an integral element in spiritual practice. Under the old paradigm—the "business-as-a-means-to-an-end" approach—some committees and task groups try to figure out how to meet as *infrequently* as possible and still get the work done. Yet when our church work becomes one of our spiritual practices, it is something we want to engage in, rather than something to avoid or simply get through.

While Vietnamese Buddhist monk, poet, and peace activist, Thich Nhat Hanh says that one smile with mindfulness is transformative, virtually all spiritual teachers agree that a spiritual practice takes time. Think of the movement that occurs within you during a relaxing bath. When you first get in it takes a while to adjust to the water temperature, to stop listening for the sounds of the phone or the kids, to stop thinking about work, to unwind. After a while, you really settle into the bath and relax, everything else floats away. Later, you become aware that the water's cooling off, that you've been away from things for a while and that it's probably time to come out. But not quite yet; there's usually one more good bit of submerging to do. And then comes the inevitable resurfacing. The same is true of a spiritual practice—it takes time to get into it, takes some time within it, and then it takes some time to get out.

Scheduling two hours for a meeting allows you to accomplish the business-work as well as attend to the spiritual-work. Longer meetings than that tend to fry people's brains and you lose effectiveness. It is far better to schedule another meeting than to go on for another hour or two.

Some congregations schedule separate meetings—one for covenant group work and one for church business. Can you imagine a church Board willingly setting aside two nights a month? Or Board members feeling deepened and fulfilled by their service rather than depleted and used up? It's happening in congregations right now.

Some congregations also schedule all—or a great many—of their meetings on one night, preceded by a potluck supper and a brief worship service. (In these congregations the ordained minister will usually spend five or ten minutes in each of the meetings rather than spending all of her time in only one.) This model not only prevents people from serving on more than one committee at a time (one way of helping people avoid overextending themselves!), it also reminds everyone that they're working together and that their work is within the context of their worshiping community.

There are three practices which, while not formal protocols, can help transform the quality of your meetings—or at least your experience of them. If consistently kept in mind, they can help the meetings flow more efficiently and keep the spirit flowing more freely.

If your meetings are like most, there's no shortage of discussion during them. Everyone who has a good idea—and even some who don't—vie for the floor. One minister remembers being a youth representative of his Presbyterian church's Board of Elders. The group engaged in a lengthy discussion about whether or not the interim minister was trying to secure a permanent position there in violation of his contract. Everyone had her or his say, some more than once. After about twenty minutes or so, the youth interrupted the other Elders and said, "Our interim minister is in the room. Why don't we ask him?" This kind of talking in order to talk—rather than in order to accomplish something—is endemic in our meetings.

It's also extremely frustrating. Have you ever returned home from a Board or committee meeting fuming that you talked and talked and talked and yet got nothing done? Many congregational leaders have left their positions—and sometimes even the church—because of this sense that it's all talk and no action. Others never even step into leadership because of this same perception.

Yet people are not, generally, simply speaking to hear the sound of their own voices. For the most part people speak up in meetings because they think that they have something important to contribute to the conversation.

It's amazing, though, what can happen when a person shifts from that perspective—"I have something to say"—to the perspective that "something has to be said."

Try this experiment. The next time you're in a meeting and you come up with a brilliant idea to share—wait. Keep your hand down and your mouth closed. Instead of piping up, look around the room. Listen. And wait. Nine times out of ten, you will soon hear that very idea coming out of someone else's mouth. Excellent! The thing that needed to be said got said, even though you weren't the person to say it. And if you can hold back from the impulse to second the thought, to express the fact that you had that idea too, the practice will be complete.

In other words, as a spiritual discipline, remind yourself that the discussion matters more than those doing the discussing. Ask yourself if what you're considering saying truly adds anything to the conversation, and then give the conversation a moment or two to help you answer the question. As a spiritual practice, meetings give us the opportunity to employ patience, humility, and faith: patience, as we wait for things to unfold rather than trying to push forward our agenda; humility, as we remind ourselves that we're not here to look good or show off our insight; and faith, as we trust that we're not the only people in the room with a good head on our shoulders and that things will move forward—maybe even more efficiently—if we're not always the ones pushing it along.

Prayerfully meditating on the agenda can help with this practice. As we look it over, certain ideas and insights will no doubt come to us. Questions will arise regarding one item; objections to something else; reasons for moving forward with a third. Make note of these things, not so that you can jump into the conversation first but so that you can make sure that they do indeed get covered, even if you're not the one to say them. One can participate fully in a meeting without uttering a word—especially when we consider our meetings to be opportunities for spiritual growth, individually and collectively, rather than merely a way of getting the work of the church done. Ironically, you'll probably find that the work of the church gets accomplished more efficiently this way as well.

In his poem "Song of Myself," Walt Whitman famously writes, "Do I contradict myself? Very well then I contradict myself. (I am large. I contain multitudes.)" And any book on spirituality worth its salt will at some point contradict itself because we, too, are large and contain multitudes. There is nothing simple about the human heart, mind, and soul; there is an unending richness and multivalent complexity to the mystery of life. The so-called spiritual life is no different. And neither is a committee meeting.

So it should not be surprising that if the previous practice might be called *hold your tongue*, it has a seemingly contradictory corollary that might be called *speak up*. There are times when you listen and wait and no one comes forth with the idea you had to contribute. In that case, speak up, even if no one else seems to be thinking as you are—perhaps especially then.

If you find yourself the only person apparently seeing things from a particular perspective, you can be pretty sure of two things: you're probably not the only person in the *congregation* to be thinking this way, and you're at this table for a reason. Perhaps you're on this Board or task force or committee precisely to speak the thoughts no one else is speaking. Again, if the purpose of this journey is to fully and deeply experience the journey itself and not merely to arrive at the destination, then too quick an arrival at the journey's "end" misses the point. And a discussion that too quickly devolves into unanimity is no discussion at all.

In one memorable instance, a congregation's Board considered entering into a financial partnership that seemed to have no downside for the congregation, yet would proffer tremendous financial benefits. After a fairly brief discussion the Board seemed to be unanimously in favor. That is, until one person spoke up and told of her misgivings about the project, her sense that this would violate the spirit of their community *as* a spiritual community. The discussion resumed, and before the night was over the Board voted unanimously, and proudly, to reject the offer. As a group they had come to recognize that the only downside to the proposal would have been the little matter that they would no longer have truly been who they said they were. They would have sold their souls, so to speak, and they had very nearly voted to do so.

One voice made all the difference. Yours could, too. So if you ever find yourself feeling that the others in the room just don't see what you see, don't understand things from your perspective, do something about it. The practice of holding your tongue is not really about not joining in the conversation but about not needing to do so *for your own sake*. When what you have to say truly adds to the conversation, speak up.

In the ongoing practice of trying to discern when each of these practices is appropriate, there are untold opportunities for growth. For some of us, speaking up is second nature and we will find great difficulty—but also great benefits—in keeping quiet. Others, though, are not accustomed to speaking their minds, perhaps worrying what others will think of them or undervaluing their own contributions—these folks will benefit from facing the challenge of speaking out. In the Christian scriptures there is a story of a rich young man who asks what he has to do to enter the kingdom of heaven. He reads the Torah and keeps its precepts, yet he feels more is needed. Jesus tells him, "You still lack one thing. Sell everything you have and give to the poor." The young man went away saddened because he was attached to his many possessions. If your attachment is to being the one who has something wise to say, practice *holding your tongue*; if your attachment is to making as little noise as possible, *speak up*.

Mission and Community

If the means are more important than the ends, from a spiritual perspective, then our intentions matter greatly. Yet congregational Boards, committees, task forces, religious education teachers, choir members, and others hardly ever spend time considering their intentions.

This is understandable, because these folks are usually pretty busy carrying out their responsibilities. They're doing their Board work or their committee work or their teaching, rehearsing, or singing, or whatever it is that they are *doing* for the church. Yet, as it says on the popular bumper sticker, "We are human *beings* not human *doings*." One wonders what it will take to get this bit of wisdom off of our cars and into our buildings.

At one level, identifying your intentions means asking why you're doing your particular piece of church work. Why *are* you discussing an alcohol use policy? Why *are* you holding another holiday fair this year? Why *are* you trying to reach a certain stewardship goal or fund this particular budget? Why are you singing this song (or singing choral music at all as opposed to rock or folk)? Why are you teaching this lesson? Why are you doing whatever it is that you're doing?

At another level, however, asking why you do what you do means asking yourselves—individually and collectively—an even deeper set of questions: Why is your congregation doing anything at all? Why does your faith community exist in the first place? What brought it into being? Why has it survived? Why is it still around and worth supporting today?

This leads naturally to a discussion of your congregation's mission statement. Not all congregations have one, of course, but a great many do. Unfortunately, few congregational members—or church leaders—even know what the mission statement is or can talk about it intelligently.

Yet if you have a mission statement, and it's a good one, it answers the macro-level question of why your congregation exists in the first place. And if you can answer *that* question, you have the answer to all those other "whys." If your congregation's life is really centered around its mission, its purpose in the world, then each and every issue that comes before each and every Board, committee, task force, and working group will relate in one way or another to this central statement.

Keeping the mission of the church in front of you may mean that certain issues will no longer be seen as appropriate to discuss. The specifics will depend, of course, on your particular mission. For example, if your congregation understands its mission as creating more justice for underserved families in your community, you may find yourself taking off your agenda items that have nothing to do with justice, families, or your local community. A church that understands itself as a "peace church" might come to realize that it's time to let go of some of its other long-standing traditions, no matter how good they are, because they do not directly support and move forward the mission. Likewise, a committee might realize that it's time to stop doing a piece of its work, now that its own mission has become more clear.

If your mission statement has helped you discover that your committee or task force has played a role in maintaining some unhealthy behaviors, what should you do about it? Consider the question as if it were asked about your family. Wouldn't you want to help your family—each of the members individually and the family unit as a whole—to become healthier? So, too, you should want to see your congregation grow stronger, deeper, more healthy, and more whole.

There may be things that you have been asked to, or have been expected to, deal with in the past that you now see are not in the best interest of the spiritual health of the church. Discuss it as a group, carefully considering how you will handle it. But remember that you are trying to break out of the habit of just doing business as usual. This applies not just to how you do the business but, perhaps, even what kinds of business you do.

The Board of one congregation, which had been struggling with money for a few years, was in a conflicted relationship with the preschool that rented some of its space. Money had always been an issue, as had difficulties of sharing space between the preschool and the church's religious education program. There was also the lingering question of whether the school, which was started by the spouse of the previous minister, was a program of the church (entitled to financial support) or a free-standing entity (needing to pull its own weight). Some Board members wanted to declare the school independent—which is how it had been functioning for years—and cut it loose so the church could find a more stable and more lucrative renter. Yet after careful consideration of its mission and its commitment to families, the Board decided to fully and formally embrace the preschool as a program of the church, to give it the financial support it needed, and to integrate it into the life of the church. The church as a whole was proud of the decision and brought a renewed spirit to the work of revitalizing "their" weekday preschool.

It doesn't always work out so nicely. Once you begin to take stands and make changes you are likely to meet resistance. This always comes with change—always. Jesus was crucified; Francis David died in prison convicted of the crime of "innovation." These things rarely happen in churches today, but people who are used to "the way we've always done things" typically aren't happy when someone starts doing things differently. Yet if you are making decisions from within this new model of leadership you won't be making them without real unanimity among the members of your Board or working group. You will really know *why* you are making them and will feel very sure about your decisions. This will not necessarily make everyone in the congregation happier about those decisions, but it will change the way you feel when faced with their displeasure.

There's another reason for undergoing this kind of transformation. The anti-racism/anti-oppression/multicultural work of the Unitarian Universalist Association has helped us to see that there are certain norms associated with individuals and institutions influenced by the dominant white, European culture. Meanwhile, a different set of norms are associated with multicultural institutions and individuals. Among the so-called "white cultural norms" include a tendency toward individualism (as opposed to collaboration and cooperation), an inward focus (as opposed to an outward focus on relationships of accountability), and a bias toward efficiency (as opposed to effectiveness and relationship).

So far we've been describing a shift from the prevailing model—in which lay leaders fend for themselves and are expected to take on too much work with too little support—to one whose main purpose is to build supportive, collaborative community, rather than this being the surprising secondary result of the "real work." Seen through a different lens, this movement represents a shift from the dominant "white cultural norm" to a "multicultural norm." Not only will transforming our lay leadership into true spiritual practice help deepen our own spiritual lives and the spiritual life of our congregations, it will also help us to, in the words of the UUA curriculum, "build the world we dream about."

One way to make this shift is as simple as reciting together your mission statement at the beginning of each meeting. (If your church doesn't have an official one, take some time within your committee or group to agree upon your own understanding of the mission of your congregation—or at least your group.) Have several copies—printed in fairly large type—distributed around the table so that they can be seen throughout the meeting. Then, as each item of business is discussed, make a point of asking yourselves, explicitly, How does this relate to our mission?

At first, it may seem hard to find direct connections. It may feel like an artificial and perhaps even a shallow exercise. Yet if you keep it alive—that is, if you engage fully with it—you will find that one of two things will happen. Either you will begin to understand the workings of your congregation in ever deeper ways, seeing how the work that you do really does reflect and support your sense of mission. Or, you will find that you stop doing certain things, because they are tangential to who you say you are, and you will begin doing other things, because you see a real need for them.

Two more of the "white cultural norms" that have been identified are either/or thinking (as opposed to both/and thinking) and operating out of a scarcity mentality (as opposed to an abundant worldview). Both of these can be seen in our propensity to defend our own positions during meetings—so quickly, in fact, that we sometimes haven't even listened to somebody's entire point before we're working out what we're going to say in response. One practice to change this behavior is to adopt the "every idea is a good idea—for five minutes" policy. This means that no one can argue against an idea for the first five minutes; everyone must act as if each idea presented is a good idea for at least a little while. Groups that have tried this report that it gives people a chance to actually listen to one another and try each other's ideas on, before simply dismissing them out of hand. You may be surprised to discover that some of these ideas actually *are* good ideas once the time limit has passed, and more people might be willing to share their ideas when they know that they're not going to be simply shot down without a full hearing.

Another difference between the two cultural norms is that the way things have been done for so long—what we might call the prevailing culture—is for people "in the know" to play their cards close to their chests. They may not intend to keep things secret—they may just be pursuing greater efficiency—yet those on the outside of those "inner circles" don't know how decisions are made, don't know what's going on, and yearn for greater "transparency." So a practice when making decisions or, even better, while having the discussions that lead to decisions, is to ask over and over again, Who else needs to know this? Ask yourself not only who *needs* to know this but who else *can* know this. At first this might seem most relevant at the Board level, yet it is applicable throughout the church.

An axiom in church growth work states, "Never do by yourself what six other people can do." It is almost certainly true that you can get most things done more efficiently by doing it yourself. And if getting it done is the main goal, then it is quite possible that you can get it done more effectively as well. But if the ultimate goal is building community and deepening your own and others' spiritual lives, then you cannot do it anywhere nearly as effectively or efficiently without help—or time.

Finally, in all things, remain curious. This is both an attitude to adopt while serving as a leader and an orientation for the institution to hold while introducing this paradigm shift. There is a classic story—told in many books about Zen and depicted in the movie *The Forbidden Kingdom*—in which a student begins going on and on about his thoughts on a particular topic. The teacher, meanwhile, pours the student a cup of tea, and keeps pouring even as the cup begins to overflow. "What are you doing?" the student cries. "The cup's already full!" "Exactly," replies the teacher. "And until you empty your own cup there's no room for any of my teaching."

Our work on the Board and committees can be very draining when it devolves into a constant series of efforts to convince others of our own opinions. We take up issues and are asked how we think and feel about them and then often strive to see that our perspective carries the day. What if we entered our meetings unsure of what we thought was the "right" thing to do or, even, of what we thought about a particular issue? Picture yourself going to a Board meeting determined first and foremost to actually learn what everyone else thought and to discover together—in and through your conversation—the correct course to take. Wouldn't this change things? In general, those who are most often delightfully surprised by the unexpected are those who, ironically, expect to be surprised.

Look for opportunities to learn more about the other people who serve with you on your Board or committee. Look for opportunities to learn more about yourself. The assumption that "we've been through this a hundred times" is really just an illusion. For the person who remains curious and who is awake to the moment, life *never* repeats itself. *This* conversation—even if it resembles others you've been involved in incredibly closely—is always a unique experience, and unique experiences are rarely, if ever, dreary or draining. The unknown, the unexpected, almost always makes us come more alive. Remember, it is the journey, not the destination, that matters most in this new way of doing church work. It is the relationships that are developed, not the items crossed off the "to do" list. It is the growth of the "fruits of the spirit" in your own life and in the congregation's life. This, ultimately, is the "why" that supersedes even the congregational mission statement—for, fundamentally, all congregations exist, as the Unitarian Universalist Association so succinctly put it recently, to be places where people can "Nurture Your Spirit; Help Heal Our World." All church work, then, is done for these same reasons.

I Put My Hand in Yours

If we update the language a little for our modern sensibilities, the metaphysical poet John Donne's famous lines sound like this: "No one is an island entire of itself; every person is a piece of the continent, a part of the main." Rev. Dr. Martin Luther King Jr. put the same idea like this: "We are tied in a single garment of destiny." The Vietnamese Buddhist monk, poet, and peace activist Thich Nhat Hanh simply says, "We inter-are."

This goes for church leaders, too.

Even if you sometimes feel as though you're out there on your own, the truth is that all the other leaders are out there with you—whether or not the patterns of your congregation encourage you to see that yet or not. Unfortunately, sometimes the power dynamics of church life will pit one group against another. For instance, the folks in religious education might think they must struggle against the social justice people for scarce financial resources or volunteers—or just the good room to meet in on Thursday night. Sometimes the choir feels as though it's shuffled around from place to place, depending on what else is happening, and so may feel a little defensive. It can be hard to open your hand and heart toward other leaders if you feel as though you're in competition with them for insufficient resources of time, talent, treasure, and turf.

Yet hopefully what you've read so far has encouraged you to understand your role as a church leader in different ways. Now it is time to look at your fellow leaders in new ways as well.

One of the challenges of serving your church community is precisely that it is, in fact, your church community. The person with whom you co-teach on Sunday morning or with whom you sit on the Finance Committee may also be someone with whom you have all kinds of other interactions. She may be someone who always hogs the conversation during the after-film discussion, or takes the best pieces of pie at the monthly suppers. Or maybe you've heard his opinions on political issues and found them troubling, or have in some other setting found him hard to be around. And yet, here you are, also serving together on the Board or task group.

Of course, this problem can manifest in the reverse manner. There might be someone with whom you are having a problem on the Board or in the choir and that problem makes it hard to socialize with her at the Spring Auction Dinner or even in the pew on Sunday morning. This overlapping of roles is one of the challenges of serving our spiritual communities.

Some Buddhist traditions teach that everyone you encounter in your life—and perhaps especially those people you find irksome and difficult—are, in reality,

Bodhisattvas who have chosen to incarnate in those particular forms to assist you on your spiritual journey. Mark Rosen's book *Thank You For Being Such a Pain* develops this notion—the people with whom we have the greatest trouble are actually, or at least have the potential to be, our greatest teachers. Think of the Fourteenth Dalai Lama, Tenzin Gyatso, referring to the Chinese who occupy his country as "my friend, my enemy." The Christian traditions, too, are filled with folk tales of people who had some encounter with a problematic stranger—often someone poor and marginalized—only to discover that this stranger was in fact the Christ, offering an opportunity to practice loving kindness and generosity of spirit.

So perhaps that bothersome Board member who seems to be always on the other side of every issue is really a Bodhisattva in disguise, providing you a lesson you need to learn. And maybe the person who always insists on following *Robert's Rules* to the letter, or never follows them, is really the Christ come to give you the chance to practice (or develop!) patience and understanding.

Taking time to get to know the people with whom you are working can be a tremendous benefit in transforming your church leadership into a deep and fulfilling spiritual practice—and not just knowing the who, what, where, and when of their lives but understanding the deeper questions about how. How do the others like to work? What are their leadership styles? How do they process information? How do they see the world?

Obviously, knowing this kind of information will help to maximize the effectiveness of your Board or committee. You'll know when certain people need extra time to process things, and can accommodate those who get easily bored by too much processing. Just as you'll know for yourself what kinds of tasks you should and shouldn't sign on for, understanding the others around you will help you *all* know which tasks bring out each of your unique talents.

In the Christian tradition, Saint Paul uses a wonderful analogy. The church, he says, is like a body. And just as a body is made up of different parts—eyes, ears, nose, mouth, hands, feet, etc.—so too is "the Body of Christ," or the body of the church. If everyone on the Board had your particular leadership style, it would be like the whole body being made up of eyes—great for seeing but not so good for hearing or moving around much. The fact that there are people on your task force or working group who are *not* like you is a great gift to the group, because it means that weaknesses in your style—and there are weaknesses in every style—will be compensated for by others who possess strengths in those same areas. And since it's unlikely that everyone in the congregation possesses the same styles or types, having a mix in the leadership increases the chances that those voices and perspectives will be represented there, too. A Board full of Promethean leaders who see no reason not to charge in, roll up their sleeves, and get things done might inadvertently overlook the Epimethean congregants, who need to take things more slowly.

At the same time, you don't need to develop some kind of quota system for personality types on every working group. For one thing, that would be highly impractical to implement. For another, not every type is suited to every task. But it does make sense to get an idea of who is who present on the Board and each committee, who has signed on and volunteered on their own. You will find that they won't be all folks of one type or another, and that's a good thing!

Having a mix of types and temperaments among the leadership—and knowing about the people with whom you are working—also benefits your own personal spiritual journey. No one of us can be all things; we cannot look at the world through all perspectives. Yet if we intentionally encounter people who experience the world differently than we do, we can increase the breadth and depth of our own way of being. Consider the opportunity to work with people of other types as a chance to flex those personality muscles. When working out, if all you ever did were seated curls you would develop strong biceps but your legs might be scrawny from lack of use. This holds true for the mind and the spirit as well—we must exercise all of our faculties if we want to nurture fully rounded growth. Working with people who are different from ourselves—perhaps even especially those who are so different from ourselves that we find them difficult—can provide us the opportunity to develop in ways we might otherwise not. Especially if we do so consciously, mindfully.

Perhaps each year the church could sponsor a leadership styles retreat for all of its leadership, or could make personality testing part of the leadership development program. Or maybe the Board and each committee could do this work on its own. In any case, taking the time to get to know one another will help you learn how to work more effectively together, enabling you to capitalize on each others' strengths while minimizing your weaknesses. It will also help you to have greater understanding of the experiences you have while working together, which is key to spiritual growth.

Some Twelve Step meetings end in a circle, with each person in turn taking the hand of the person next to them and saying, "I put my hand in yours, so that we may do together what I cannot do alone." Such a ritual reminds the group of its common need of one another. What if your meetings ended this way? You could use this quotation, of course, but could also use the church's unison affirmation, a favorite poem, or the group could compose some new, original words each year. Imagine the impact of hearing such words, month after month, meeting after meeting. It could be powerful indeed—a reminder that you are not isolated individuals but a community, working together for the common good of your congregation, and the world beyond your walls.

Let us assume that the lessons of this book so far have been put into place in your congregation. You and your fellow leaders have taken a look at yourselves and each other and know something about how you understand leadership and the kinds of leaders you are. Having done so, you've come to recognize the power of the diversity among you—not only for the work of the church but also for your own personal spiritual journeys. And now you've also come to see that the various kinds of work are being done in appropriate ways—that committees are doing committee work and that others have been freed to do the work that they like to do. (Even if this isn't the case throughout your congregation but is happening—or beginning to happen—in the committee or task group that you're involved with, this is a great thing.)

There is still one more thing needed to help foster a culture in which providing leadership can be a real opportunity for spiritual growth and development. Many congregations today are experimenting with the development of small group ministries—groups of eight to twelve people who meet regularly (monthly, or even weekly) to engage in deep personal connection with one another. In evangelical churches, where this concept originated, these groups are not limited to adult education programming—they are part and parcel of everything the church does. So, the Finance Committee would understand itself as a small group ministry that gathers not to discuss a poem but the church's budget. In some of these churches, there is a Landscaping Small Group, and the choir sees itself as a small group as well. Even the professional staff does not just have "staff meetings" but meet as a small group of church staff.

We can adopt this practice in our congregations as well, and it is the natural next step toward understanding that it is not the outcome that matters most but the path taken toward that outcome.

Some congregations have moved in this direction by making sure that a significant portion of their agenda is dedicated to activities that will help deepen the connections among members. Some of these activities were discussed earlier—the check-in and check-out, beginning with opening words that are chosen by different members of the group, designating someone as the vibes-watcher, and lighting a chalice at the start of the meeting. Each of these elements devotes part of meeting to the business of attending to the relational needs of the committee and not just the business. They put community building and nurturance on a par with decision making and action steps.

Other congregations take a different tack. Instead of, or in addition to, taking time within a committee meeting for community building, their committees attend worship together at least once a month and then the members go out to brunch with their spouses as a way of deepening interpersonal connections. This reminds them that they are linked to one another not only because they serve together on a committee but because they are part of a wider church community. (And the inclusion of spouses expands the circumference of their circle.)

In other congregations, committees and working groups attend extra meetings each month to facilitate this deeper kind of bonding. The Board meets twice a month, for example—once to do the work of the church and once to build community together. This may be difficult to believe for Board members operating under the old paradigm. After all, in many congregations these meetings are a cause for dread, so the thought of intentionally adding another one is inconceivable! Yet congregations that have adopted this practice generally have found it to be extremely well received.

This is because what is being suggested here is not more of the same. Just adding new elements to these meetings, like a check-in, or more commitments for the members, like monthly brunches after church or additional meetings, would be insane if that's all there was to it. A popular definition of insanity is to do the same thing over and over again and expect different results. Likewise, doing the same thing along with a few extra things added in and expecting big changes as a result would be insane too.

Instead, what's being suggested here is nothing short of an "Apostles in Rome" situation, a "turning the world upside down" proposition. When Jacob awakes from his dream in the Biblical book of Genesis and has his realization that "surely God is in this place" he sees that place in a new way. No longer is it simply the dusty side of the road where he'd had to sleep with a rock for a pillow. Now it is a holy site, worthy of an altar to his Lord. He even gives it a new name and, according to tradition, it is the spot on which the great Temple is eventually built.

So too, Moses, when he encounters God in the burning bush. Even with such a miraculous vision he must be told to remove his shoes "for the place where you stand is holy ground." He apparently didn't recognize it as such at first. But when, as E. E. Cummings puts it, "the eyes of his eyes were opened," he saw not only that spot but the whole mountain in a new way. His whole life was changed. When you begin to see your leadership as a part of your spiritual practice, these meetings will become a different place for you, these encounters will be changed, and so these additions will not be simply "more of the same" but rather something entirely new.

Let's return for a moment to our new assumption that what really matters is not whether or not we get through our agenda but how we attend to it, that it's not how much we accomplish but the quality of the meeting. The focus shifts from asking, What needs to get done? to asking, What is happening right now?

In a standard small group ministry (or covenant group), the group might begin with a reading and a chalice lighting, and then have a check-in and a discussion. It might be focused on another, longer reading. It might center around a book that's being read in common, or a film everyone's seen, or a series of questions the facilitator poses. Yet always the intent is for the discussion to come back to the questions, What is this bringing up for me? Where does this connect in my life? What does this have to do with my own spiritual journey? This makes small group ministry different from a book club or a movie discussion group, which might allow the discussions to stay more outwardly focused on the topic itself.

It is possible—although it seems like a stretch at first—for the Finance Committee to take up its work on the budget with the same attitude as small group ministry. While considering the details of next year's budget, for instance, and how the results of the current stewardship drive might impact next year's programming, members of the committee could ask themselves what feelings are coming up for them. How do the numbers affect them personally, and how do they relate to how they feel about their church home? Rather than this being a distraction, when you think of your service to the church as a spiritual practice this becomes one of the primary purposes of your work together!

Yes, the budget has to be prepared. And it will be. But consider that one of the reasons that church finance work can feel so hard is driving to get the budget prepared at the cost of attending to our feelings about the process. "This is our church," we say. "It shouldn't be like this here." And yet we perpetuate the conditions that make it "like this" over and over again.

Perhaps it is time to fundamentally change what you're doing. Perhaps rather than trying to see how much busy-ness you can cram into an agenda, you could see how much space you can maintain in it and then allow that space to be filled by real human interactions—the kind you have come to church for in the first place. The work will get done—it always does. In the end, if it takes longer to do it this way, but you don't burn out, you get more people involved, and the entire quality of the experience increases dramatically—wouldn't that be considered a gain?

There are certainly personality types who will be driven to distraction by "processing feelings" as opposed to accomplishing tasks. Luckily, you will now be far better known to one another in these ways, and you can make accommodations for one another's temperaments. And there will always be some tasks that are just that—tasks that need to be done.

This is not a mandate from On High for a new way things must be done; it is an encouragement to an attitudinal shift. So it is important that even the implementation of these ideas be done *relationally*, because that's what this chapter has been all about.

If this new paradigm is imposed—if it is just one more thing expected of you—you will have missed the point. Instead, try the more difficult but, in the end, far more essential (that is, of the essence) route of *being* your way into these new ways of relating to one another. Again, the work will get done. It may—undoubtedly will—take longer than it often has in the past. But perhaps the reason you're reading this book is that something has not been working with the way you've been doing things before. It may be time to try something new.

As you get to know one another as leaders and as people—members of the same faith community and same human family—it is natural for bonds of affection to develop. You may not always like all the people who serve on the Board with you; some of the other religious education teachers may strike you as not exactly your cup of tea—but don't be surprised if you find your heart warming to them. You might consider developing ways to actively support one another. Some people add the other members of the committee on which they serve to the list of family and friends for whom they pray each day. Others take note of important days like birthdays and anniversaries and make sure to send a card or bring muffins to the meeting closest to that day. Each person will find his or her own way of showing it, but making a regular, disciplined practice of demonstrating to the other leaders that you care will deepen the experience of working together.

Bringing It All Together

By now you may have noticed that there are no special practices described in this book. Rather, there have just been examples of ways to put the key ideas into action. Each of these, though, could be taken up as an intentional practice.

None of these suggested actions depends on any particular understanding of the nature of reality—the atheist and the Zoroastrian could equally apply any of them. Certainly, though, if your own religiosity provides you with practices that are meaningful, these could be added to this list. Keep in mind that if the only place you're attending to the spiritual dimensions of your life is in your work as a church leader you will probably still burn out. For there is no such thing as a "spiritual dimension" to your life. Spirituality is not one thing among many that make up who we are. It is a way of looking at the world, a point of view through which everything we encounter passes. Time on a meditation cushion, in a crowded sanctuary, playing with your kids, and discussing the church's budget are all spiritual activities if the spiritual mindset is active. If not, you could live your life in a monastery located on a ley line with no benefit.

The challenges and invitations suggested in this book can be adopted by just one person or by a group of church leaders. Certainly, on your own, you can go a long way toward making your leadership role spiritually fulfilling by engaging with the kinds of personal practices described here. You might even find that as you transform your relationship with the work of the church that others will do so as well.

People may begin to notice that you're not getting as frustrated or confused as they are, or that you're the one who always seems to know just how to sum things up, or that when you're at the table the meeting always seems to be informed by the spirit of the congregation. They may begin to ask you what your "secret" is. And they will almost certainly begin to ask you to take on ever greater leadership. And you, holding your "no" as sacred as your "yes," will make wise choices and continue to model engaging leadership as a spiritual practice.

Yet, you will be able to go much further in this direction if the rest of your Board or committee are looking at things this way as well—if everyone takes the time to reflect mindfully on meetings past and the meetings to come as preparation; if all of you agree that you will discern when to hold your tongue and when to speak up; if you come to an agreement about taking time out to breathe when the situation demands it; and if you all approach your work with a spirit of curiosity and openness.

Finally, these three observations about the spirituality of church work may help encourage you along the way:

It makes sense to see church leadership as a spiritual practice because church leadership is hard. An old quip goes that leading a group of Unitarian Universalists is like herding cats; another one says that trying to get a decision made in one of our meetings is like trying to nail gelatin to the wall. And then there's the joke, "Where three or four Unitarian Universalists have gathered you'll find four or five opinions."

It's not that difficult to get people talking about the grueling labors undertaken by this Stewardship Committee or that Search Committee or by your church's Board during one particularly difficult period in the church's history. Simply put, coming to understand and experience church leadership as a spiritual practice can be an antidote to this unhealthy dynamic. It makes it possible for lay leadership to become not simply a means to an end but an end in itself, not just a way to keep things going but a way to do what you came to church for in the first place—to deepen your spiritual life, make deeper connections with others, and make a difference in the world. Rather than being a path to burnout, it can be a road to enlightenment! Traditionally, world religions describe their spiritual practices as bearing such fruit as patience, joy, love, generosity of spirit, wisdom, insight, compassion, courage. What if this is how people felt when they came off their term on the Board?

Church leadership is a spiritual practice because the church is a spiritual institution. Churches are not small businesses, no matter how much they resemble them in some respects. And while it may be useful to think about them in these ways at times, it is vitally important to remember that they are also not social service agencies, schools, or theaters. Our congregations are spiritual communities. Therefore, they should maximize their opportunities to see with spiritual eyes. At their best, churches can be—perhaps should be—a kind of spiritual total immersion environment. And just as total immersion language programs make no distinction between classroom time and non-classroom time, so too, congregations can avoid distinguishing between spiritual and non-spiritual things. From the pastoral prayer to the passage of a policy it's all a school of the soul.

Perhaps this is one of the reasons that church work is sometimes difficult in the first place. When we attend a dry-as-dust meeting at work we usually don't suffer too much angst because we don't expect anything else. It is work, after all, and we expect it to feel like work. Yet when it's our *church*, our spiritual home, there's often a nagging voice saying "it shouldn't be like this." It shouldn't feel like work there; it should feel spiritual, yet it doesn't. And so a feeling of dissonance builds up, making us feel anxious and irritable and a host of other negative emotions.

Learning to see our church work as part of our spiritual work, actually *making* it so, is one way to resolve this dissonance and create more harmony within our church community. That voice that says "it shouldn't feel like this here" is actually on to something, and recognizing the spiritual nature of church work is not just a new catch phrase, it's a reorienting of our understandings. After all, that's what religions have always done, what spirituality always does—reorient our vision to new ways of seeing things. This is why it's so important that this is not just lip service or a new set of things to do in the meeting. This is about a new way to do the things we're doing—the practices are merely tools to help reinforce this perspective.

Using the spiritual lens deepens and enriches our lives. Henry David Thoreau famously said that he did not want, when it came to be time for him to die, to discover that he had not truly lived. He said that he did not want to waste his time living what is "not life," but rather to devote himself to being as fully and as wholly (one might say holy) alive as possible. Different religions have different ways of describing what this "life that is life" is all about and why most of us don't live that way most of the time. Some talk about our being asleep. Others talk about our being deluded. Others talk about our being dead, not truly alive. Others talk about our not being aware.

Yet all agree that the way to wake up, or become aware, is to pick up and use the spiritual lens as often as possible, to see that all is sacred and that we are part and parcel of it. This, it seems, is at the core of all religions, when their idiosyncratic particularities are stripped away. Buddhists, Christians, Jews, Muslims would all agree—once they got past their differing languages for it—that the universe in which we live, and of which we are a part, is truly awesome and wonder-filled and that we come fully and truly alive when we recognize that and live out of that recognition. As Jesus is remembered as saying, "the Kingdom is here, among you." Or, as the Buddha said, "Everything is perfect, just as it is." Even humanists have found their ways to say it. Engaging church leadership as a spiritual practice provides us one more opportunity to use this spiritual lens and learn the lessons it has to teach.

Through the spiritual lens, we see for ourselves that there is no place where God is not, just as Jacob discovered in the Jewish story of Jacob's ladder. Through his dream Jacob both literally and figuratively awoke to the realization, "Surely the Lord is in this place and I did not know it."

The Christian mystic Meister Eckhart wrote, "If I could spend an hour with the lowliest of God's creatures—say, a caterpillar—I would have no need of sermons." Anything can be a Bible, a Qur'an; anywhere can be a Temple, a Zendo. If you can find the sacred at a church Finance Committee meeting around budget time, you can do it anywhere! Seeing church leadership as a spiritual practice gives us one more tool to open our eyes, our minds, and our hearts to the depths of life so that we might more deeply live and love and be in tune with life's depths—and in this way find our lives and our living transformed.

Resources

Alexander, Scott, ed. *Everyday Spiritual Practice: Simple Pathways for Enriching Your Life.* Skinner House Books, 2001.

Bandy, Thomas G. *Kicking Habits: Welcome Relief for Addicted Churches.* Abingdon Press, 2001.

Bass, Dorothy C., ed. *Practicing Our Faith: A Way of Life for a Searching People*. Jossey-Bass Publishers, 1998.

Heller, Anne Odin. *Churchworks: A Well-Body Book for Congregations.* Skinner House Books, 1999.

Moore, Thomas. *A Life at Work: The Joy of Discovering What You Were Born to Do.* Broadway Books, 2008.

Olsen, Charles M. *Transforming Church Boards into Communities of Spiritual Leaders*. Alban Institute, 1995.

Robinson, Anthony B. *Transforming Congregational Culture.* Wm. B Eerdmans Publishing Company, 2000.

Trumbauer, Jean Morris. *Sharing the Ministry: A Practical Guide for Transforming Volunteers into Ministers.* Augsburg Fortress Publishers, 1995.

Online Resources

Lay Leadership Training

The Alban Institute, www.alban.org

> This is a well-respected, ecumenical think-tank that offers training and resources on a wide variety of church-related topics.

The Unitarian Universalist Association, www.uua.org

> The UUA has a variety of essays, articles, curricula, and other resources on a vast array of subjects relevant to church leaders of all kinds and is well worth a look. It has everything from nuts and bolts details to theoretical and theological reflections to how to run effective meetings to anti-racism/anti-oppression/multicultural initiatives.
>
> In addition, each UUA district offers its own programs of lay leadership development, including day-long intensives and week-long leadership schools. Some are for current leaders, some for people considering leadership; some are for youth, some for adults. There are both local trainings and regional ones for which neighboring districts collaborate. Some of these programs have been around for decades; oth-

ers are being developed as this book goes to press. Contact your district office—or visit its website—to find out what your district offers.

Personality/Leadership Styles

For more information about some of the more popular personality type and leadership style inventories, check out these websites:

DiSC Personal Profile System, www.discprofile.com

Keirsey Temperament Sorter, www.keirsey.com

The Myers & Briggs Foundation, www.myersbriggs.org

Acknowledgments

The great Christian mystic Meister Eckhart said that if you could pray only one prayer in your lifetime and it was "thank you," it would suffice. I have so much to be grateful for:

First and foremost, I am grateful for those glimpses I have had of that Unnamable Mystery that keep me looking, and grateful that that "transcending mystery and wonder" revels in revealing itself in delightful and surprising ways.

I am grateful to and for my children, Theo and Lester —divine grace made manifest—who have made my heart grow beyond anything I'd imagined, and who've opened my eyes to the reality of miracles.

I want to thank my wife and best friend, Mary, who has grounded me and lifted me up, and reminded me that these things are real.

I would say "thank you" to the laypeople in the congregations I have served, who have shown me both how challenging and how rewarding serving the church can be. (My clergy colleagues have shown me this too, of course.) I want to thank those people who, through their lay service, have discovered a calling to the ordained ministry; those who have discerned a calling to the ministry of professional religious education; and those who have heard a calling to continuing ministries of lay leadership. Each and every one of the people I'm thinking about (and I hope you know who you are) has demonstrated to me the meaning of ministry and the power of listening to a calling. I hope I have been able to do the same. (I would particularly thank David Kolb who, when president of the First Universalist Church of Yarmouth, Maine, taught me the phrase, "Your 'no' is as sacred as your 'yes.'")

I am grateful to those with whom I share the ministry of spiritual direction (as well as the good people of the Shalem Institute who trained so many of us), who remind me to keep the "spiritual lens" if not actually in front of my eyes at all times, at least close at hand.

I'd also like to thank the author Richard Bach, in whose book *Illusions* I found the wisdom, "You teach best what you most need to learn." Without this, I'd never have had the chutzpah to write books about spirituality.

And last, but quite far from least, I want to thank the folks at Skinner House, who believed I had another book in me, most especially Mary Benard, who so gently and so generously works the magic that turns a writer into an author, and Marshall Hawkins, who carried me over the goal line.

To you all, and to so many others unnamed but not forgotten: thank you. I hope it will suffice.